이슬의 비밀

조무근 · 조병은 사제 영역 동시집

동시 **조무근**
영역 **조병은**

소년문학사

영역 동시집을 엮으며

동시는 모든 시詩의 기본이 되는 글로서 이 세상에서 가장 순수하고 아름다운 문학입니다. 그래서 나는 평생 동심 속에서 살아오면서 아동문학 중에서도 동시만을 고집스럽게 써 왔으며 써 나갈 것입니다.

지금부터 10여 년 전, 초등학교 졸업시킨 지 30년 만에 만나 사제 간의 인연으로 지금까지 내 동시를 영역英譯해 준 조병은趙炳銀 교수가 고맙기 그지없습니다.

조 교수는 미국 대학에서 영미문학과 영시를 전공하여 박사 학위를 받은 재원으로서 훌륭한 제자를 두어 큰 영광입니다.

경상도의 마산과 창원, 거제, 포항 등지에서 40여 년간의 떠돌이 생활을 청산하고 고향이기도 한 강릉에서 요양생활을 하면서 이틀에 한 번꼴로 혈액투석을 하고 있습니다. 독서와 글

쓰기로 지루한 투병생활의 고통을 참아내게 된 것도 치유의 한 방법이라 자위하며 매사에 감사한 마음으로 지내고 있습니다. 지난 연말 내 고희 기념으로 출간하려 했으나 여러 사정으로 지금에야 발간하게 되었습니다.

10여 년간 『소년문학』에 「이 달의 영작시」로 연재한 것을 한데 묶어 사제 영역 동시집을 내게 되어 더욱 뜻이 깊습니다.

소년문학사 서정환 사장님과 박갑순 편집장님께 감사드리며, 이 동시집이 지구촌 시대 모든 어린이들에게 꿈과 희망이 되기를 바랍니다.

2011년 가을에

조무근

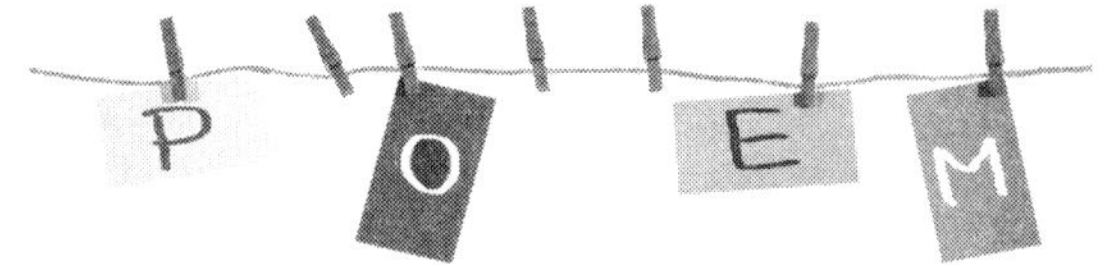

제1부 상모를 돌리는 등댓불

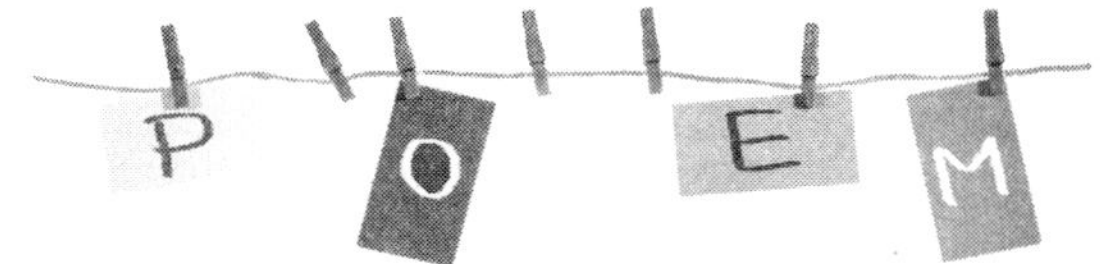

제2부 덕유산 현장학습

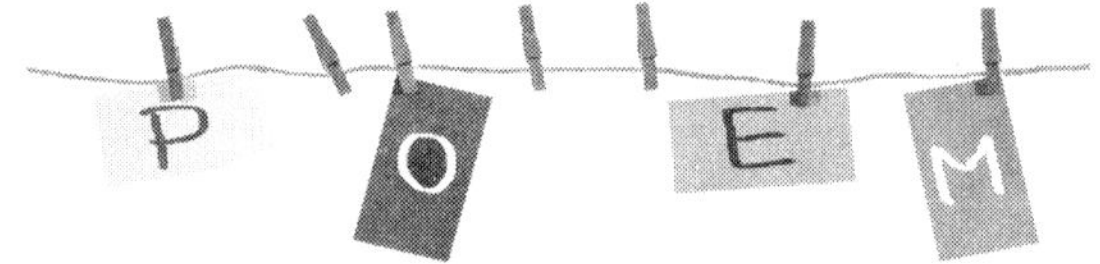

제3부 오징어 빨래

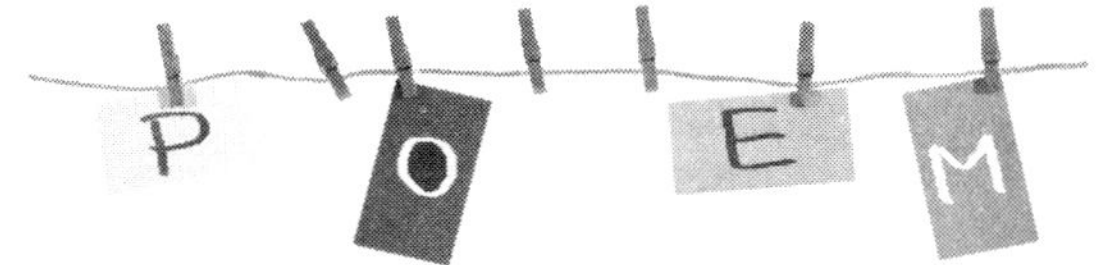

제4부 비 오는 날의 연잎은

제 1 부

상모를 돌리는 등댓불

소나기

마구
우산을 두드린다

알록달록 오색 우산
멋진 타악기

후두둑
후두두둑……

소나기 쏟아지는 날만
골라잡아 열리는
난타 연주회

The Shower

It rumbles
the umbrella.

The colorful umbrella
Becomes a wonderful percussion instrument.

Tapping, tapping,
ta-tapping,

A drum concert
Held only
on a showering day.

새벽안개

추한 것은
다 덮었다

새벽은
아직 깨지 않았는데

차라리
모든 허물
덮어주고 싶다

겨울나기 준비하는
쇠오리 떼
화들짝 놀라 사라지고

그 틈바구니엔
마을 풍경
희미한 수채화로 남아 있다

Dawn Fog

It covered
all ugly things,

The dawn
is not fully awaken yet.

It rather
wishes to hide
all faults.

Flocks of ducks
that prepare for winter
Fly away, being surprised.

In-between,
The rural landscape
Remains as a dim(misty)water color.

저녁연기

정이월
바람 자는 날
건넌방 군불은
언제나 내 차지

두 손으로 연기를 헤집으며
발 동동 구르며
기침하며 취한다

흙담 굴뚝에서부터
낮은 데로 번져
뒤란 장독대를 돌다 지쳐서
매화나무 등걸에서 쉬면
하얗게 벙그는 매화 꽃송이

아련히 들려오는
재 넘어 기적소리
문득 그리움으로 피어오르는
한 줄기 저녁연기

Evening Smoke

On windless days
Of early January and February,
I am in charge of
Extra heating of the room beyond.

I clear away the smoke with two hands,
Stamping my feet,
And coughing, being intoxicated.

The smoke spreads down wards
From the clay-walled chimney.
It curls around the bean pots on the backyard and being tired,
It takes a rest on a stubble of an old plum tree,
Blooming the plum-tree flowers into white smiling.

At the sound of train heard far away from the hill,
A string of evening smoke
Suddenly flares as a reminiscence.

이슬의 비밀

한 방울
두 방울
모이면

동그란
고 모양
늘 그대로

세상은
조그만
하나의 지구본

너와 난
항상
하나가 되는
동그란 사이.

Secrets of the Dew

One drop,
Two drops,
Together

A round drop
As round
As ever

The world is
A small
Globe.

Your and I
Always
Become One
In such round friendship.

병과 바람

'누가 함부로 버렸나?'
'지나치다 한 번 들러봤지.'

"어!
병 속에 빗물이 들어갔나?'

빈 병 속으로 들어간 바람
그만 술에 취해

부웅
부우웅~

트림을 한다

A Bottle & the wind

Who there it away?

I dropped by when I was passing.

Aha!
Is it the rain water that is in the bottle?

The wind that went into the empty bottle
Was drunk.

Burping, burping,
Bu-burping,

It is belching.

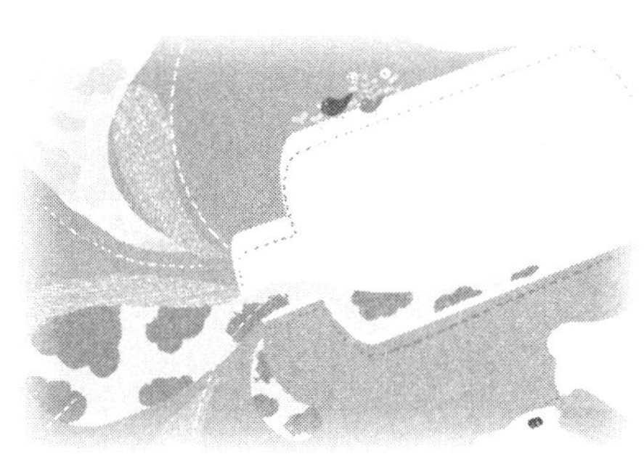

파도 (1)

조약돌 널려 있는
여름 바닷가

밤새도록
홑이불 걷어차며
잠꼬대 소리

덮어 주면 또다시
돌아눕다가

알몸 조약돌
부끄런 줄 모르고
밤새도록
터뜨리는
티 없는 웃음소리

The Waves (I)

The summer coast
With pebbles scattered around.

All night long,
Throwing off the bed sheet
They are talking in sleep.

If you cover them with a sheet
They turn over again on their side.

Naked pebbles,
Having no sense of shame,
All through the night
Are cracking into
An innocent peal of laughter.

파도 (2)

파도는
하루 절반
햇살을 먹는다.

햇살이 눈부시는
낮 파도는
하얀 이 내놓고
티없이 웃고 있다.

파도는
하루 절반
별빛을 먹는다.

달빛이 반짝이는
밤 파도는
금물결처럼
아름답고 잔잔하다.

The Waves (II)

The waves
Eat the sunlight
Half of the day.

Dazzled by the sunlight
The day waves
Showing their white teeth
Are smiling a spotless smile.

The waves
Eat the starlight
The other half of the day.

Twinkling with the moonlight
The night waves
Just like a golden ripple
Are beautiful and calm.

상모를 돌리는 등댓불

상모를 돌린다
깜깜한 밤바다에서

열두 발 끝에 야광등 달고
신나게 상모를 돌린다.

밤 파도 넘실넘실 덩달아 춤추고
별 친구 반짝반짝 응원도 하고

밤바다 주인공 되어
밤새도록 상모를 돌린다.

열두 발 끝에 야광등 달고
이리 저리 바닷길 밝힌다.

The Beacon Lamp that turns Sangmo

It turns Sang-Mo[1)]
In the dark sea of the night.

It turns Sang-Mo with excitement,
Hanging nightglow lamplight at the end of its twelve-fathom strip.

The nightly wave dances aiong.
The star-friends cheer up, twinkle, twinkle.

Becoming a hero every night.
It turns Sang-Mo all through the night.

Hanging nightglow lamplight at the end of its twelve-fathom strip.
It lightens up here and there of the way of the sea.

---

1) High Cap With a Long Strip.

더위 예보

열대야로
잠을 설쳤는데

새벽부터 매미는
자지러지게
울어댄다.

'오늘 또
무척 찌겠군.'

Heat Forecast

Last night, I could not sleep
Because of the tropical heat.

From early dawn,
Cicadas give shrill cries.

'We will have another scorching day today.'

산에서 배워요

산새들 아무리 조잘대며 떠들어도
산골물 아무리 수다떨며 흘러도
산은 그저 말없이 귀담아듣고는
아빠의 의젓한 맘 산에서 배워요.

아무리 높은 산도 작은 산과 어깨동무
수많은 나무들은 풀숲과 어울리고
철마다 형형색색 손수 옷을 갈아입혀
엄마의 자상한 맘 산에서 배워요.

We Learn From Mountains

However chatty the mountain birds chirp.
However noisily the streams run,
Mountains listen quietly without complaints.
We learn taciturn father's dignity from the mountains.

However high the mountains,
They are putting arms around each other's shoulder with small mountains.
Many trees become friends with the undergrowth,
Changing clothes in various colours each season.
We learn tender mother's love from the mountains.

엉덩방아 찧는 빗방울

땅바닥에 떨어지는 빗방울 좀 살펴 봐
엉덩방아 찧고서도 웃는 꼴이 재밌잖아
냇가로 강 바다로 제 갈길 가는 것도
또로롱 똑똑 또로롱 똑똑 빗방울로 떨어져서
다시 만나 반갑다고 엉덩방아 찧는다

땅바닥에 떨어지는 빗방울 좀 살펴 봐
엉덩방아 찧고서도 웃는 꼴이 재밌잖아
아지랑이 떠돌다가 빗방울로 떨어져서
또로롱 똑똑 또로롱 똑똑 빗방울로 떨어져서
다시 만나 반갑다고 엉덩방아 찧는다

Raindrops that Fall on Their Buttocks

Look at the raindrops that fall on the ground.
Isn't it funny that they laugh, falling on their buttocks?
Each going its own way to the stream, to the river, or to the sea,
Falling as raindrops, drop, drip, drop, dropping, drip, dripping,
They fall on their buttocks, being glad they meet again.

Look at the raindrops that fall on the ground.
Isn't if funny that they laugh, falling on their buttocks?
Floating as veil of heat shimmer,
Falling as raindrops, drop, drip, drop, dropping, drip, dripping,
They fall on their buttocks, being glad they meet again.

가을의 무게

주름살 투성이 은행나무
여름 내내 넓혔던 그늘에다
노오란 잎사귀 떨군다
노오란 방석을 편다

그 큰 방석에다
아랫목 만들려나 봐

서둘러 겨울을 준비하는
참 푹신한
가을의 무게

참 아름다운
가을의 무게

The Weight of Autumn

An all-wrinkled ginkgo tree
Falls down its yellow leaves,

Unfolds a yellow cushion
On the shade
It has spread all Summer.

Perhaps, it puts a warm floor
On such a large cushion

The Weight of autumn
How very fluffy it is,
Preparing for winter in a hurry

The weight of autumn
How very beautiful it is.

빛의 가르침

(1) 직진

'사람답게 살아야 해.'

아버지는
내 어린 날
한 줄기 빛이셨습니다.

(2) 반사

거울 앞에서
매무새 훑어보면
비뚤어진 내 맘까지
알려줍니다.

어떤 내 모습이 바른가
고쳐줍니다.

(3) 굴절

'쓸데없는 고집
그만 부려.'

양보하고 타협하는 마음
가져야 한다고
내 고집불통 꺾어 놓습니다

Lessons of the Light

(I) Going Straight

'Live a life worthy of man.'

My father was a streak of light
In my childhood.

(II) Reflexion

In front of a mirror
Looking over my attire,
It shows my perverse mind.

It corrects my behavior,
Telling what is right.

(III) Refraction

'Don't be unnecessarily stubborn.'

Telling me to have
A considerate and compromising attitude,
It makes me yield my stubbornness.

제 2 부

덕유산 현장학습

참 묘한 선생님

일학년 때 선생님은 참 순한 선생님
아무리 꾸중해도 무섭지 않아요.
선생님은 모두 다 친절하다rh 믿었죠.
참 순한 선생님이 난 제일 좋아요.

삼학년 때 선생님은 참 엄한 선생님
꾸중은 없었지만 무섭기만 했어요.
선생님 앞에서는 아무 말도 못했죠.
참 엄한 선생님 땜에 올바르게 자랐죠.

오학년 때 선생님은 참 묘한 선생님.
무서울 때 숨 한 번 제대로 못 쉬고
어떤 때는 부모처럼 자애로웠죠.
무섭고도 순한 선생님 난 제일 존경해요.

A Very Mysterious Teacher

My teacher in the Primary first was a very mild teacher,
Whom I was not afraid of, however he scolded.
I believed that all teachers were kind.
A very mild teacher I like best.

My teacher in the Primary third was a very strict teacher.
Though not scolded, I was scared.
I could not say a word in front of him.
Thanks to such a strict teacher, I grew up a good boy.

My teacher in the Primary fifth was a very mysterious teacher.
When scared, we hardly had a breath;
Other times, he was as affectionate as my parents.
The strict and mild teacher I respect most.

조약돌 친구야

고만고만한 내 또래
조약돌 친구야.

발가벗고 한데 얼려
미역감던 친구야.

우리들 사이엔
못할 말이 없었지.

마음까지 동글동글
다정스런 친구야.

고만고만한 어릴 적
조약돌 친구야.

졸졸졸 시냇물처럼
귓속말 친구야.

우리들 사이엔
아무 비밀 없었지.

모나잖은 우리 사이
그리운 친구야.

To a Shingle Chum

To a shingle chum
Who are of even size and age with me.

You are the one
Who used to swim stark naked with me.

There was
no secret between us.

What a sweet friend you are
With a mind of all round!

You are a shingle chum
of even size with me.

A friend whispering just like a bróok
Murmuring along.

There was never a secret between us
Nor an odd behavior between us.

Oh, chum!
I miss you so much.

아이구, 내 새끼야

입학식 날 엄마 손 잡고
처음 학교 다녀 오면

할머니는 대문 앞에서
"아이구, 내 새끼야."

두 손 벌려 덥석
안아 주셔요

방학 맞아 오랜만에
시골 아빠 고향 가면

할머니는 동구 밖에서
"아이구, 내 새끼야."

이빨 없는 웃음으로
반겨주지요.

Oh, Dear My baby!

When I come back from the first day of school,
Hand in hand with my mom.

My grandma, in front of the gate, calls
"Oh, dear my baby!"

And hugs me
in both bands.

When I visit my dad's hometown in a long time
In my vacation,

My grandma, at the entrance of the village,
"Oh, my dear baby!"

Greets me
with a toothless smile.

빈집 같은 집

또래 형제들
하나만 빠져도
빈집 같다 말했죠
우리 엄마는

엄마가 하루만 집 비웠는데
왜 그리도 허전할까요?
우리들은

열쇠 목걸이 한 아이만 봐도
걔네 집은 보나마나
빈집.

A House like an Empty House

If one brother about the same age is out,
"It's like an empty house."
My mom used to say.

My mom is not at home even one day,
Why is it felt so empty,
For all of us?

A kid necklaced with a key,
Tells for sure that his house is empty.

시골버스

출발도 제멋대로
도착도 제멋대로

언제 어디든
정류장 따로 없이
제멋대로 태워준다.

구불구불
흔들흔들

출발도 도착도 제멋대로
시골사람 빼닮았다.

Country-running Bus

It starts when it likes,
It arrives as it pleases.

It stops where and when it likes,
Regardless of the bus stop.

It blows a horn once more
Lest country people miss the bus.

On the winding road,
Swinging from time to time.

It starts and arrives as it pleases.

Just like the country people.

이름 대신

이율곡, 이퇴계
진짜 이름인줄 알았는데

이이, 이황이라는 진짜 이름보다
더 멋지게 불렀었구나.

“203호야, 노올자.”
“누구니?”
“나야 나, 903호야.”

요즘엔
모든 이름
아예 숫자 투성이.

In the Place of Names

Yi, Yul-Gok, Lee, Toe-Gye,
I thought they were real names.

But they were called more often
Than the real naves, YI, Yi and Lee, Hwang.

“Hi, Number 203. Let‘s play.”
“Who are you?”
“It's me. Apartment number 903.”

These days, all the names are
replaced by numbers.

엄마의 공짜 사랑

"엄마, 요즘 인기 있는 메이커 운동화 사 줘."
"신고 있는 신발 아직 멀쩡한데 신발타령이니?"

종이쪽지 건네주고 도망치듯 등교했다.

— 엄마가 빚진 것
심부름 값 : 2,000원
쓰레기 치운 값 : 1,000원
집안 청소한 것 : 1,000원
기타 : 1,000원
합계 : 5,000원

저녁식사 후 내민 엄마의 하얀 봉투
빳빳한 천 원짜리 다섯 장과 편지

— 아들이 엄마에게 빚진 것
자장가 불러준 값 : 공짜
생일잔치 열어 준 값 : 공짜

아플 때 간호해 준 값 : 공짜
아들에게 주는 사랑 값 : 공짜
합계 : 없음

너무나 부끄러워
5천 원 모두 엄마 손에 쥐어 주고 다짐했다.

'조금도 꾀부리지 않고
시키는 대로 뭐든지 할게요
물론 공짜로.'

Mom's Free Love

"Mom, please buy me a fashion sneaker with famous brand."

"Your sneaker is still ok. Why all this pressing for shoes?"

I handed a slip of paper to my mom and ran away to school.

- Mon owes me;

For making errands : 2,000won

For recycling : 1,000won

For cleaning : 1,000won

Others : 1,000won

Total : 5,000won

After dinner, mom gave me a whine envelop,

Five new 1,000won bills and a letter in it.

- My son owes me;

For singing lullaby : free
For holding a birthday party : free
For nursing when ill : free
For loving my son : free
Total : free

Too ashamed,
I put all the 5,000won in mom′ s hands,
And made up my mind :

"I will do whatever you want me to do,
Without any negligence,
Of course, for free."

덕유산 현장 학습

삼도봉에서
살짝 몸을 틀어 바라 봐
지리 공부가 될 거야.

저쪽은 충청도 영동과 금산
이쪽은 경상도 김천과 거창
여기는 전라도 무주

신라 사람들이
수없이 드나들었다는
나제통문

덕유산 가는 길은
역사 공부도 되고

봄에는 철쭉
여름엔 피서
가을엔 단풍
볼거리도 많은 곳

참, 궁금한 게
하나 있지.

덕유산 자락
무주 구천동에는
구씨와 천씨 성을 가진 사람들
아직도 전설처럼 살고 있을까?

Field Work at Mountain Deok-yu

Slightly turn your body at Samdo peak and look,
There you can study geography.

Yungdong and Keumsan in Chungcheong province to that direction,
Kimcheon and Keochang in Kyungsang province on this side,
And here, Mu-ju in Jeolla Province.

Na-je Gate of Entry, through which people
Numerously came in and went away in the
Silla Period.

The way to Mountain Deok-yu
Teaches us history as well.

With royal azaleas in spring,
Cool shades in summer,
Colored leaves in autumn,

There are many objects of interest and sightseeing places.

By the way, I am curious to know:
In the Kuchundong, Mu-ju,
Do people with surnames of Ku and Chun
Still live there as was said in the legend?

동그란 욕심

보름달은 큰 소망 딱 하나 있지요
사랑을 덩어리 채 주고 싶어서
밝은 빛만 골라 모아 뭉쳐 뒀다가
해마다 정월 보름 골라 잡아서
동그란 온 세상을 밝혀줘요

보름달은 큰 소망 딱 하나 있지요
아이들이 두 팔 벌려 원을 그리며
누구 것이 더 큰가 자랑하고파
해마다 팔월 보름 추석날 맞춰
둥글게 큰 입 벌려 한바탕 웃음줘요.

A Round Desire

The full moon has only one big wish:
It wants to give love as a whole,
Chooses only the bright lights and gathers them,
Waits for every January 15th, the lunar full moon day,
And lightens the whole round world.

The full moon has only one big wish:
That children stretch their both arms to make a circle,
Want to compete and boast whose circle is bigger,
It waits for August full moon every year,
And gives a good laugh with its mouth wide open.

연탄

긴 겨울 밤 까만 연탄이
하얀 연탄재 되기까지

양말과 운동화 말리던 부뚜막
아랫목 장판 검게 눌어도
연탄의 추억으로 추위를 녹였지

일생을 마친 연탄재가
얼어붙은 골목길에 뿌려져
미끄런 길 막아주던 작은 배려
그 얼마나 고마우냐

남 위해 아낌없이 나눠주는
연탄의 한 살이
그 얼마나 위대하냐

The Briquet

Long winter night,
Until the black briquet
Became white briquet cinder.

Socks and sneakers were dried
On the kitchen range.
Until the lower floor was scorched black,
We warmed ourselves
With the body temperature of the briquet.

How grateful the small consideration
It showed!
When the briquet cinder was spread
On the narrow icy lane of the village,
And prevented us from slipping.

How great the life cycle of a briquet is!
That gives itself away for others to the last moment.

집게손가락

엄지와 검지 대신
집게손가락이란 이름으로
우린 언제나 함께했지

전화기나 텔레비전 다이얼
돌리면서
누르면서
검지만 도맡아 일해 오다가

엄지는 형님으로
검지는 동생으로
모든 일 리모컨으로 척척
편한 세상 되었지만

족집게 손가락 옛 명성
함께 일하던 그때가 그리운 건
어쩐 일일까.

Forefingers

Instead of a thumb and an index finger,
We have worked together all the time
By the name of forefingers.

Of pushing the telephone numbers and
Turning the TV dial,
Only the index finger was in full charge.

The thumb, an elder brother,
The index finger, a younger brother,
Although now the remote controller made a convenient world,
In changing 야민 and numbers.
Why is it that
We miss the old reputation of forefingers
And the time when we worked together?

계단

우리 매일
계단 오르내리며
살아가고 있지요

둥지 같은 아파트도 드나들고
육교나 지하도를 지날 때도

지금까지 오르내린 계단
하나로 잇는다면
도대체 그 높인 얼마나 될까
앞으로 얼마나 올라가야만 할까

단번에 서너 칸
올라갈 수 없는 계단

오늘도 나는
한 칸 한 칸을
로봇처럼 오르내리고 있다

Stairs

We live everyday
Mounting up and down the stairs.

Coming in and going out the nest-like apartments,
Passing the subways or the suspended ways.

If we line up and spread the stairs
We have mounted up and down,
How high it might reach?
How many more stairs yet to mount?

No three or four steps at a time for anyone,
Today, I mount up and down the stairs,
Step by step,
Like a robot.

징검다리

닿을 듯
말 듯한
거리

마음은
언제나 가깝다.

재조갈
시냇물 얘기
귀담아 듣다가

간지럼타는
돌다리
까르르-
웃음 쏟아놓고

개울 사이
이 마을
저 마을
웃음이 오간다.

Stepping Stones

A distance that one may reach
Or may not.

It is near in mind, thoubh.

Listening to the stories of the water and the pebbles.
Stepping stones are tickled-
'Chuckle, chuckle'

They burst into laughter.

Through the villages on each side of the stream.
Laughter comes and goes.

허물 벗은 집

허물 벗은
매미의 빈집 좀 보렴.

한여름 고 짧은 시간이라도
맘껏 노래 부를 수 있었던 건
허물 벗은 집 덕분이라고
말하고 싶구나.

제 몸뚱이에 꼭 맞는
아주 작은 집
무슨 세간이 필요하랴.
그저 아무 욕심 없이
마지막 내 모든 허물까지
털어버린 자국.

허물 벗은
매미의 오막살이 좀 보렴.

Cast-off House of a Cicada

Look at the cast-off empty house
Of a cicada!

For such a short time in mid-summer
That the cicada could sing to its full
Was all thanks to the cast-off house,
I'd like to say.

A house as tiny as to fit for its body,
What more furniture would it need?
A mark of casting off even the last slough
Without any greed.

Look at the cast-off hut of a cicada, please!

제3부

오징어 빨래

쇠똥구리

참
이상한 일도 있지

지저분한 것만 골라
경단 만들어 굴리는 건

지구가 둥글다는 걸
실험하는 걸 거야.

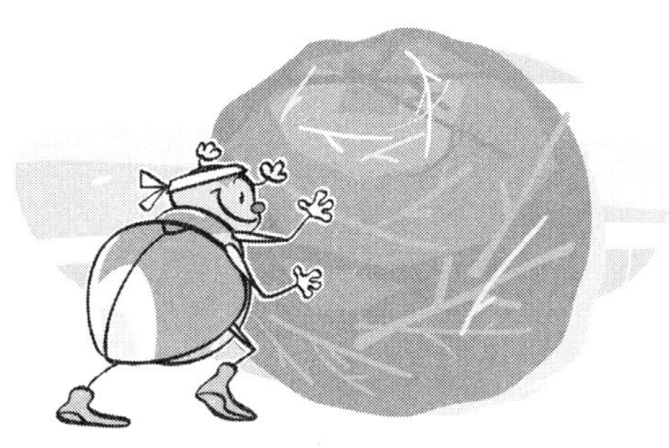

새김질로 짓이겨낸
그 쇠똥 속에서
참을성까지 배우네.

제 몸집보다 큰 경단
같이 구르면서도
지구를 데리고 노는 것 좀 봐.

Dung Beetle

Wow, how strange it is!

That a dung beetle chooses all dirty dung,
Makes round rice cake dumplings,
And roll them around.

Perhaps, the dung beetle is experimenting
That the earth is round.

From the cowdung douht
That the dung beetle makes by rumination,
We learn patience, too.

When it rolls around allong with
A big round rice cake, bigger than its body,
Look, how it is playing with the globe!

달팽이

초롬한 풀숲에서
풀잎의 단잠 깨우는
또 하나
파아란 세상이 열린다.

언제나
모든 일 서두름 없이
조심조심 한 발 내디디는
의젓한 네 몸짓.

별들의 속삭임도
와닿는
두 뿔 안테나.

외로울 듯
외로울 듯
외로움 돌돌 말아
신비한 우주 얘기
저만이 안다.

Snail

When the leaves of grass are
Awakened from a sweet dream,
In a green grass-forest,
One more green world is open.

Always
Without hurrying in anything,
Taking a step by step with care and care
Your gesture is as mature as it can be.

An antenna on two cheeks
On which the murmur of the start
Is resched and heard.

As if lonely,
As if lonely,
They roll the loneliness
Into mysterious tales of the universe,
That only they can understand.

참 아름답구나

(1)
저무는 산골짜기 풀섶에
산국, 감국, 구절초, 쑥부쟁이
가을꽃 한데 어울려
향기 밴 저녁놀
참 아름답구나.

(2)
산기슭 이어진 밭자락
누렇게 말라버린 잎 사이사이로
다북다북 붙어 있는
잘 익은 콩 꼬투리
이삭 무게 못 이겨 축 늘어뜨리고
그 위에 내려앉아 수수알 쪼아 먹다
인기척에 후루룩 날아가는 참새 떼
참 아름답구나.

(3)
오염된 도랑에서 더러운 것 다 먹고도
꿋꿋이 피어나는 고마리 풀
더더욱 아름답구나

So Beautiful!

(I)

So beautiful is the evening sky
Bearing fragrance of autumn flowers,
Various mums, wild flowers, all together
Among the grass of dusky valley.

(II)

The well-ripened bean-pod
That are closely lined among the yellow dry leaves,
On the furrow that leads to the foot of a mountain.
The loaded shear bending its head
Over the flocks of sparrow that feed on the com,
And fly away at human voice,
They are so beautiful.

(III)

The Korean persicary that blooms firmly,
Absorbing all dirts in a contaminated brook.
It is the most beautiful of all.

생명 발견

엄마,
모든 게 살아 있어. 그치?

그래.
바람 불면 숲이 살아나고
나무가 살아나는 거야.

해 지면 밤이 살아나고
해 뜨고 아침이 살아나지.

소리 지르면 메아리가 살아나고
흙을 만지면 흙이 살아 있다는 걸
손으로 직접 느끼잖아.

정말, 그렇구나!
무엇이든 건드리는 대로
느끼는 대로 다 살아나는구나.

Life Discovery

Mon,
Everything is alive, isn't it?

Yes,
At the blowing wind, the forest becomes alive.
And so do the trees.

When the sun sets, the night revives,
When the sun rises, the morning gets alive.

When you shout, a cicada becomes alive, and
When you touch the soil, you can feel it alive.

Yes, indeed!
Whatever you touch,
Whatever you feel,
All become alive.

오징어 빨래

동해안 갯마을에 겨울철 돌아오면
오징어 빨래들 덕장마다 널렸어요
오-라 참 이상한 빨래도 있군 그래
짭조름한 갯내음에 군침돌며 말라요

동해안 어촌마을 어디서나 볼 수 있는
오징어 빨래들 바닷바람 손짓해요
오라 참 재밌는 빨래도 있군 그래
덜 말린 오징어는 군것질감 피데기

The Squid-Laundry

When winter comes around in the mud-flat county,
On the Eastern coast,
The squid-laundries are hung in every fish rack.
O-ho, What a strange clothesline it is!
Drying at the salted smell of the mud-flat,
Watering our mouth.

The Squid-laundries which can be seen any fishing village
On the Eastern Coast,
Wave their hands at the sea winds.
O ho, What interesting laundries, indeed!
The less-dried squids are good snacks between meals.

안테나

'오늘
파도가 무척 세겠는 걸.'

안테나 눈 곧추세워
귀 기울여 알아맞히는
바닷게 좀 봐.

'오늘
소나기 한 차례 쏟아지겠는 걸.'

안테나 더듬이 곧추세워
일기예보 알아맞히는
달팽이좀 봐.

Antenna

'Today,
we will have big waves.'

Look at the crab,
With its antenna-eye upright
It forecasts, listening with attentive ears.

'Today,
we shall have a round of shower.'

Look at the snail
That forecasts the weather
With its antenna-horns straight.

간지러워요

산골짝 계곡물이 급하게 흘러
바위 틈새 옆구리를 간질러 놓고
키드득 키드득 웃음 참지 못해요.

간지럽다 간지러워 계곡물이랑
간지럽다 간지러워 바윗돌들도
서로서로 배꼽 쥐고 한바탕 장난쳐요.

바닷가 몽돌밭에 파도가 치면
또래 돌들 떠밀어서 간질러 놓고
차르르 차르르 웃음 참지 못해요.

간지럽다 간지러워 파도결이랑
간지럽다 간지러워 몽돌 또래도
서로서로 쳐다보며 한바탕 수다떨죠.

It'S Tickling

The stream water of the mountain valley runs in a hurry,
Tickles the side of the crevice in the rock,
And cannot suppress its laugh, giggling, giggling.

'It′ s tickling, very tickling' the stream water,
'It′ s tickling, very tickling' the rock stones,
Play a round of trick, holding each other's bellybotton.

When the wave beats upon the shore of shingles,
Tickling other shingles of the same size by pushing them,
It cannot suppress a laugh, grating, grating.

'It′ s tickling, very tickling' the curb of waves,
'It′ s tickling, very tickling' the shingles of the same size,
Looking at each other, they enjoy a good chat for a spell.

길 (1)

길을 간다
실핏줄처럼 얽힌 길을

새들은 자유롭게
하늘 지름길로 날고

등짐 진 달팽이는
긴 여행길

자벌레는 제 몸뚱일
재면서 가는데

살아 있는 건
모두 다
제 갈 길 있는 걸까

오늘도 나는
실핏줄 미로를 헤맨다

질러서도 가봤다가
돌아서도 가 봤다가

The Road (1)

I go along the road,
A road entangled like blood veins.

Birds fly on the shortcut of the sky
A snail on its thorn sets off a long journey.
A worm goes with its body as a scale

All living things have their
own ways to go.

Today I wander among the maze of blood veins,
Trying a short-cut,
Or taking a detour.

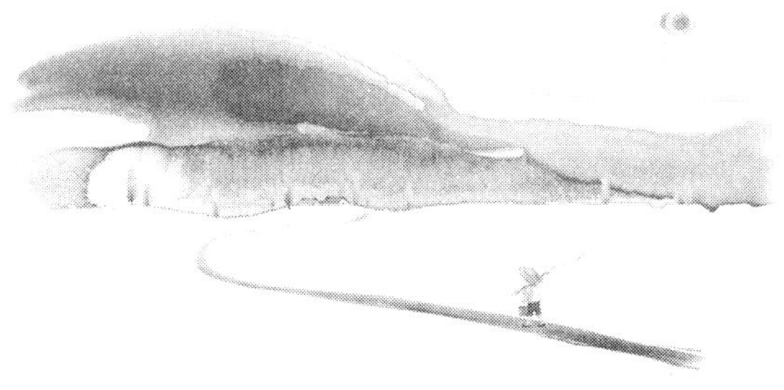

길 (2)

옛날부터
사람들이 하나둘씩 모이자
길도 덩달아 생겨

길은 길끼리 이어져
핏줄을 이루고
어디든 통하죠

실핏줄은 오솔길
큰 핏줄은 고속도로

피가 온몸 돌아 흐르듯
드나드는 그 길로
어김없이 다니고

그 길을 통해
사람과 사람
마음과 마음이 이어져
지구촌 이루지요.

The Road (2)

From ancient times, people gathered one by one,
So did appear the road, too.

A road leads to another,
Forming a blood vein,
And passes throuhg anywhere.

A fine vein is foot path,
A wide vein is a high way.

Like blood that circulates the body,
People keep the exact road
When they come and go.

Through the road,
Aman is linked to another man,
A imnd to another mind,
Making a global town.

하늘 지름길

신호등이 필요없다
새들이 맘대로 날아다니게
직선 길 터 준다.

별똥별이 제 몸 사르며
밤하늘에다 직선을 긋는다
누가 뭐라 하든
제 갈 길 간다.

연이 제멋대로
하늘을 쏘다닌다
연줄이 잔소릴 늘어놓아도
제 할 일 하고야 만다.

언제나
지름길 열어주는 하늘

언제나
하고픈 거 하도록
자유를 주는 하늘.

A Short-Cut in the Sky

No need of traffic signal
It opens a straight line
For the birds to fly as they want

A falling star draws a direct line
Across the night sky, burning its own body.
It oges its own way whatever ohters say.

A kite floats around the sky.
It finishes its work however the string nags.

The sky that always
Opens a short-cut.

The sky that always
Gives freedom to do what they want.

뻘밭 운동장에서

썰물이 빠져나간 바다는
뻘밭 운동장

필요 없는 신발
양말도 벗어던지고
바지 걷어올린 채
맨발로 맨발로
뻘밭 거닐어 봐.

발바닥 발가락 사이 사이로
간질이는 말랑말랑한
갯벌의 감촉

발가락 통해
지구를 웃기려나 봐.

지구야
간지럼 타는 지구야!
한 번 씨익 웃어 볼래?

On the Mud-flat Playground

The sea on the ebb
Makes a mud-flat playground.

Taking needless shoes
And socks off,
With the end of trousers rolled,
In bare and bare feet,
Let's take a walk on the mud-flat.

On the bottom of the foot and between the toes,
The tickling, and soft
Feeling of the mud-flat.

By tickling the toes,
I t may want to tickle the earth.

Dear Earth,
Dear ticklish earth,
Will you show us a quick smile?

하늘을 청소하는 빗자루

강바람은 하늘 향해
구름을 청소하는
빗자루 갈대

좀 더 높은 곳 향해
흰 머리칼 날리며
하늘을 청소하는
빗자루 억새

갈대와 억새는
하늘을 청소하는
할아버지 환경 미화원

The Broomstick that Sweeps the Sky

The river wind against the sky
Sweeping the clouds,
Is a reed broom.

Higher and higher,
Fluttering its white hair,
Sweeping the sky,
Is a eulalia broom.

The reed and the eulalia
Are broomsticks
That sweep the sky.

씨감자 (1)

동글동글
잘도 생겼네.

온몸에 돋아난
점. 점. 복점.

그 복점 씨가 되어
씨감자 되었나.

씨눈 살점에서
다시 싹 트는 건
봄 땅속 체온 때문이야.

귀한 생명 나눠주신
그 정성으로
땅속 열매 복덩이들
주렁주렁 열릴 테지.

Seed Potato (I)

Being round,
It is good-looking.

Breaking out all over the body,
A spot, a spot, a mark of good fortune.

Then, did the mark become a seed?
And has become a seed potato?

New sprouts again from the embryo,
All because of the temperature of the spring soil.

Thanks to such devotion
With which it is sharing its precious life,
The blessed lumps in the soil
Grow in full bearing.

씨감자 (2)

아무 감자나
씨감잔 될 수 없지.

한결같이 튼실하고
잘생긴 감자.

씨감자 하나에
씨눈은 여럿
거기에서 싹이 돋잖아.

외눈 살점 떼어내야만
싹이 돋아
덩이덩이 감자알 태어날 테지.

외눈 살점 떼어낸
그 아픔만큼 얻어지는
감자 농사.

농사만큼은
그냥 얻어지는 법
절대로 없단다.

Seed Potato (II)

Not all potatoes
Can become seed potatoes.
Only those both strong and good-looking can.

Several embryos for each seed potato,
And new sprouts from them.

By cutting off the only flesh eye,
The seed sprouts and
Lumps and lumps of potatoes will be growing.

The harvest of potatoes as much as the pain
They go through.

Never comes anything from nothing
In agriculture.

제4부

비 오는 날의 연잎은

나무는

나무는
깊숙이 뿌리내려야만
쓸모있는 재목감 된다지.

나무는
하늘 높이 자라야만
튼튼한 재목감 된다지.

도대체 우리네 꿈은
얼마나 큰가
또 얼마나 깊은가

우리도 꿈나무처럼
높이 가지 뻗게 하자
깊이 뿌리내리게 하자.

A Tree is

A Tree,
Only when it roots deep,
Can make itself a useful log.

A Tree,
Only When it grows as high as the sky,
Can make itself a strong pillar.

How deep on earth is our dream,
And how big.

Let us stretch the branches of our dream
As high as the sky,
And plant the roots of our dream
As deep as the tree.

나무가 아프면

나무가 아프면
어떻게 하죠?

바람이 이따금
이마 어루만져 주고

산새들 부리로
맥박도 재 보고

하루 한 번씩 들르는 해님
오늘 기분 어떤지 표정 살피며
체온 재고 가면서

때로는 보슬비로
열 내려 주고

혹시 감기라도 들까 봐
나뭇잎 떨구면서
긴 기도에 잠긴다

If a Tree is Sick

If a tree is sick.
What shall we do?

The wind feels its head
From time to time.

The mountain birds take its pulse
With their bills.

The sun that visits once a day
Watches its facial expression, leaving
After checking its temperature,
Often cools its high temperature
With drizzles.

Then it absorbs itself into a long prayer,
Falling the leaves of the tree,
Being afraid if it catches a cold.

나무들의 수화手話

5월 아침 숲길 거닐어 봤니?
말은 않지만 나뭇잎들은 저희들끼리
눈치로 수근대잖아.

이리저리 얽혀 있는 길섶 칡넝쿨도
손짓으로 통화중인가 보다.

겨우내 움츠렸던
산새들의 재잘거리는 노래

나뭇잎들도 산새처럼 노래하고 싶어
수화를 하면서
입만 뻐끔뻐끔

Sign Language of the Trees

Have you ever walked on a woodland path in May morning?

Although they do not speak,
The leaves of the trees are whispering among themselves
Using signs.

The arrowroot vines at the road side
May communicate with one another
By hand gestures.

The twittering of the mountain birds
That have shrunken all winter long!

Longing to sing like the birds.
The leaves shape their lips,
Using sign language.

섬 백리향

오죽했으면
이름까지 백리향일까.

울릉도 나래분지
푸르스름한 풀에까지
향기가 뱄다.

덩굴에 매달린
볼품없는 작은 꽃망울
터질 무렵
온통 섬 전체가 향기 가득.

백리향처럼
이웃마다 향기가 풍길 수 있다면…

가슴에 손 얹고
혼자 중얼거려 본다.

부끄러운
나.

Island Thyme

What a befitting name!
It is called a 'scent that spreads around 100-li distance'.

In the Narae Basin on Wool-rung Do Island,
Even the green grass is soaked blue with the scent.

Though unimpressive tiny flower bud
Hung on a bine, Around the time it bursts,
How full the scent spreads all through the island!

Just like the thyme,
I wish we could spread out our fragrance to our neighbours.

With my hands pressed on my breast,
I murmur to myself.

How ashamed I am!
Without missing even one time.

제비꽃

노란 개나리꽃
빨간 진달래꽃이
봄의 전부인 양 착각하지 마.

한 번쯤 쪼그려 앉아
들길에 핀 작은 아름다움도
볼 줄 아는 아량 좀 가져 봐.

우린 사실 너무나도
높은 곳만 바라보고 왔잖아.

참 이상도 해라
해마다 봄이 올 무렵이면
누가 뭐라 하든 간에
발 아래 작은 아름다움을
어김없이 많이들 피워 놓거든.

Violets

Yellow forsythias,
Pink azaleas,
Don′ t mistake them for all of spring.

Be generous and squat for a time
To appreciate the little beauty
Blooming on a path of the field.

We have too much looked upon
High places, haven′ t we?

How mysterious it is!
That by the time spring comes,
Though nobody cares,
Look the little beauties under the foot
That have numerously bloomed!
Without missing even one time.

연잎 마당

연잎 마당에서
구슬치기 한다.

비 오는 날 골라잡아
구슬치기 한다.

<u>또르르르</u>……
<u>또르르르</u>……
하얀 웃음 굴리면서
구슬치기 한다.

연꽃 등 아래
연잎 마당에서

Lotus Garden

They roll the glass beads
In the lotus garden.

Have chosen a rainy day
For rolling the beads.

Rolling over and over,
They roll the glass beads.
Rolling a white laughter

Under the lotus lamp,
In the lotus garden

비 오는 날의 연잎은

빗방울은
연잎에만 떨어지면
옥구슬이 됩니다.

연잎은
빗방울이 많다 싶으면
몸을 기울여
귀한 구슬들은 쏟아 버립니다.

가질 만큼 가지고
그 이상 되면
미련없이 버립니다.

그렇게
마음을 비웁니다.

Lotus Leaves on a Rainy Day

Raindrops,
When they fall on the lotus leaves
Become jade beads.

Lotus leaves,
When they think that they have too many raindrops,
Lean their bodies
And pour away the precious beads.

They take only as many as they need
And give away what extra raindrops,
Without lingering desire.

As such,
They empty their minds.

느낌표로 서 있는 미루나무

마을 들판에
키다리 미루나무

들판 도화지에
느낌표로 서 있다.

봄 여름에는
연초록색

가을 들판에선
황금빛으로

겨울 들녘에
맨몸으로 쓸쓸히 서 있다.

계절따라
색 느낌표로 바꾸면서
서 있는 미루나무

A Poplar,
An Exclamation Mark

In the field of a village
A daddy longlegs poplar.

In the drawing paper,
An exclamation mark.

In the autumn,
In golden color,

In the winter,
In bare and lonely body.

Changing the colors of exclamation mark
At the change of seasons,
The poplar is standing tall.

고정관념을 깨는 꽃

(1)
'해바라기야,
큰 시계 갖고 있다고
너무 뽐내지 마.'

어둠 밝히는 달맞이꽃
새벽이 돼서야 꽃 피우는
나팔꽃 좀 보렴
고정관념 깨고
멋지게들 살아가고 있잖아.

(2)
벌 나비만
꽃가루 옮겨
가루받이하는 줄 아니?

소나무 같은 바늘잎 나무들

그리고 은행나무와 옥수수는
바람이 가루받이 도와 주잖아.

또한 벌새, 동박새는 물론
연꽃은 물이
가루받이를 도와준다는 구나.

모두들 저 나름대로
고정관념 깨면서
멋지게들 살아가고 있는 것 좀 봐.

Flowers that Break Fixed Ideas

(I)

'Hi, sunflower!
Don't brag too much that you have a big watch.

An evening primrose that lightens up the darkness of night,
And please look at the morning glory
that blooms as late as the next dawn.
They are having a wonderful life,
Breaking our fixed ideas.

(II)

Know only bees and butterflies
pollinate carrying pollens?

For the needle-leaf trees like a pine tree,
And a ginkgo-tree and a corn stalk,
Wind helps their pollination.

Likewise, as for a lotus
As well as a bee-bird and a camellia-bird,
Water helps their pollination.

Look at them
All who lead a wonderful life of their own.
Breaking our fixed ideas.

광합성 작용

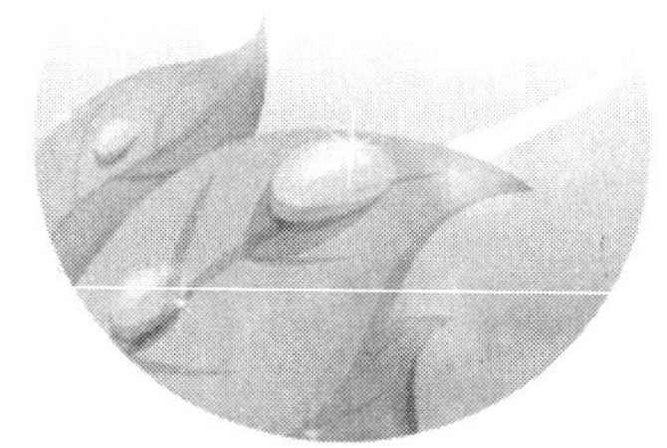

손바닥 손금 보듯
나뭇잎 좀 펴 봐

잎맥이 실핏줄처럼
참 많이도 퍼져 있네

햇볕을 받아
뿌리에서 길어올린 물로
이산화탄소와 반죽해
양분 만드는 일
다 잎에서 한다면서….

연둣빛 느낌표를
수없이 찍어내는
나뭇잎 손바닥

잎은
식물의 보물창고라며…….

Photosynthesis

Spread the leaf,
As if looking at your palm line.

The leaf veins lay spread out
Like blood veins.

The tree takes in sunshine,
Drays water from its root,
Mixes water with carbon dioxide,

And makes nutritional food,
Doing everything in the leaf, they say…….

The leaf-palm
That presses numerous light green
Exclamation marks.
The leaf is the plant's storage of jewels,
You say.

겨울 태백산

눈꽃 뒤집어쓴
주목 무리들
그대로 조각작품이다

눈길 등산로에서
어린 시절로 돌아가
엉덩이 눈썰매를 타면

살아 천년
죽어 천년

눈꽃 인
주목 조각품 사이로

그대로
태백산 지키는
신(神)

Winter Taebaek Mountain

A group of yew trees bloomed snowflakes.
Sculptures as they are.

On the climbing track,
Going back to childhood,
I try hip skiing.

Thousand years in living,
The same thousand in death.

Among sculptures
Wearing snowflakes on their heads,
The mountain God
Keeps guard on Taebaek Mountain.

눈꽃나무

눈꽃모자 쓴
겨울나무

눈부시도록
하얀꽃 피웠네

내 어릴 적
물동이 인 어머니

A Tree With Snowflakes

A winter tree
In the cap of snowflakes

Bloomed
A dazzling white flower.

My mom with a water pot on her head
When I was a little kid.

눈 내린 날에

눈이 내렸다.
하얀 속살까지 드러내놓고

모나거나
날카로운 모든 것
둥그렇게 두툼한 흰 옷 입히고

자잘한 허물까지도
감싸주면서
바르게 살라고 한다.

뽀드득뽀드득
눈을 밟으며

때로는
마음의 때까지 벗으란다.

On a Snowy Day

We had snow.

It had fallen
Showing its white bare body.

It had all sharp, edged things wear into
Round thick white clothes.

Embracing even small specks of weaknesses,
It advices us to live a good life.

Treading on the snow,
'Crunch, crunch.'

It urges us to remove
All the stains in our minds.

금강소나무의 장례식

태풍 루사 때
백수를 누린 금강소나무는
쓰러져 돌아가셨습니다.

덩굴손이 수의로 입혀지고
알록달록 버섯 꽃상여를 꾸며
장례를 치릅니다.

시신 주변 뱀돌며
개미 떼의 긴 행렬
조의를 표합니다.

워낙 귀하신 몸이라
일년장으로 하나 봅니다.

귀한 자손도 남겨서
복받을 거라며
금강소나무를 산신으로 모십니다.

Funeral of Pinus densiflora for. Erecta

When the Typhoon Rusa rushed upon,
The hundred-year-old Pinus densiflora for. erecta tree
Fell down and passed away.

With an ivy-shroud covered the body,
With its hearse decorated with colorful mushrooms,
A funeral ceremony was held.

Circling around the body,
A log train of ants
Showed their condolences.

Of such a high status,
They had a burial in one year's period after death.

With the noble offspring left behind,
Thinking they were blessed,
They honored it as the god of mountain.

조무근曺茂根 선생님은

1941년 함북 성진에서 태어나 강릉에서 성장하였습니다.

강릉사범과 경희대학교에서 공부하였습니다.

강원도 · 경남 · 경북에서 공·사립 초등학교에서 41년간 근무하고 2000년에 포항제철 지곡초등학교 교감으로 퇴임했습니다.

1979년에 『매일신문』 신춘문예, 아동문학평론지 동시 추천 완료, 『월간문학』 신인상에 당선되었습니다.

한국아동문학작가상(1979), 영남아동문학상(1993), 황조근조훈장(2000) 한정동아동문학상(2008), 교육부장관상(3회), 글짓기도상(5회) 등을 받았습니다.

저서로는 동시집 『하늘을 도는 굴렁쇠』(1979), 『동그란 욕심』(1983), 『허물 벗는 아이들』(1989), 『꿈나무들아』(1996), 『허물 벗은 집』(2000), 『질러서도 가 봤다가 돌아서도 가 봤다가』(2003), 『자연의 버릇』(2006), 『엉덩방아 찧는 빗방울』(2009), 『이슬의 비밀』(2011) 등이 있습니다.

그리고 위인전 5권, 세계명작 2권, 전래동화 5권, 독서와 글짓기(이론서) 등도 집필했습니다.

한국문인협회 회원 및 경북지회 아동분과 회장과 국제펜클럽 회원 및 경북지역위원회 부회장, 한국아동문학연구회 경북지부장 등을 역임했습니다.

또한 색동회 포항지회 창립회장을 역임했고 현재 고문으로 활동하고 있습니다.

현재 신장 장애 2급으로 이틀에 한 번꼴로 혈액 투석으로 투병 중입니다.

현재 한국문협 및 펜클럽 회원, 한국아동문학회 중앙위원, 한국아동문학연구회 운영위원, 한국동요음악회 작사분과 회원, 강원문협, 강릉문협, 관동문학회, 동시문학회 회원이며 솔바람 동요문학회 회장입니다.

조병은 선생님은

강원도 강릉에서 태어났습니다.

강원대학교와 서울대학교, 미국 북텍사스 대학원에서 영어교육학과 영문학을 전공하고 영문학 박사학위를 취득하였습니다.

1995년부터 성공회대학교 영어학과에서 영미문학과 영시를 가르치고 있습니다.

2002~2003년에는 영국 윈체스터 대학교에서 1년간 초빙교수로 지냈습니다.

주요 연구업적은 로버트 브라우닝의 극적 독백에 관한 박사학위 논문을 비롯하여 영국 19세기 낭만주의 및 빅토리아조 시인들 및 현대 영미시인들에 관한 연구 논문 및 영어교육에 관한 논문이 있습니다.

그리고 몇 편의 영한, 한영 번역서가 있습니다.

Byung-Eun Cho

Was born in Kang-Neung City, Kang-Won do, Korea.

Studied English Education at Kangwon National University(B.A.), English Literature at Seoul National University(M.A.), and English Literature at University of North Texas, USA(Ph. D).

Have been teaching English Poetry, Novel and English Literature in general, at Sung-Kong-Hoe University in Seoul since 1995.

Visited England as a Visiting Professor at Winchester University, Winchester, UK, during 2002~2003.

Had various research papers on the 19th Century English Poets including Robert Browning, William Wordsworth, Percy Shelley, Matthew Arnold, and Christina Rossetti; on Modern English poets including T.S. Eliot, Philip Larkin and Seamus Heaney; and on Teaching English as a Foreign Language.

Had some translations in both Korean into English and English into Korean about literature and theology.

조무근 · 조병은 사제 영역 동시집

인　　쇄 / 2011년 10월 10일
발　　행 / 2011년 10월 12일

지 은 이 / 조 무 근 · 조 병 은

펴 낸 이 / 서 정 환
펴 낸 곳 / **소년문학사**

출판등록 / 1984년 8월 17일 제28호
주　　소 / 전주시 태평동 251-30
전　　화 / (063)275-4000, 252-5633
전자우편 / sina321@hanmail.net

값 10,000원

ISBN 978-89-5925-912-0 73810